To purchase framed prints of cartoons or to license cartoons for use in sites, periodicals or other media, please contact rja825@aol.com or aragonpublishing@aol.com

That legendary "simple country lawyer" turned US Senator, the late Sam Irvin of North Carolina, once said that "an ounce of humor is worth a ton of erudition." That aphorism has the ring of truth about it. Humor also has an inoffensive, non-threatening way of illuminating our foibles, our inner-most vanities and our imperfections.

The best kind of humor is that which takes an ordinary, everyday event and reveals its latent absurdity by tilting it ever so slightly to one side or another, or by using substitution or exaggeration, or even playful heresy.

This collection does not focus on lawyers because they are more vulnerable to the weightless arrows of humor than are doctors, businessmen, eminent statesmen, politicians or even our cultural luminaries. Lawyers are no different from these other professionals or the rest of us.

When humor is good natured, as is our intention, it can humble us without humiliating us; it can prevent us from taking ourselves too seriously and even make us laugh at ourselves. In short, it can be good for the soul. This is the spirit in which this and future collections poking fun at other professionals have been conceived and rendered.

A personal note: Though I found my MBA-driven business career both rewarding and fulfilling, there has always been a part of me that would have loved the life of the Law.

Robert J Aragon
May 2011
Los Angeles
fromheretoabsurdity.com

"As the Executor, I've been asked to read this Last Will and Testament to all members of the immediate family."

"I'll see you in Court!"

AMBULANCE
TORT LAW
ARAGÓN & GUERREROS-©

"Something about this jury really bothers me...I just can't put my finger on it."

Ms. Melissa vanden Heuval, Esq., meticulously prepares her clothing argument.

"Where was I on the evening of July 23rd at precisely 11:47? EVERYWHERE!"

"...then Scotty sez, 'Let's go get that damned cat!' I didn't say nothin'...I didn't do nothin'...it was all Scotty's idea!"

"Can you believe it? The Senior Partner was barking orders at me all morning."

"Your Honor, the Jury believes that as a lesson to he and others which may follow, the Defendant should be sentenced to death."

"Objection! Your Honor, the Jury's sentence of death is grammatically incorrect!"

"Let me remind you, Mr. Holmes, that you are under oath and ask you, once again: Did you or did you not use cocaine as alleged by Dr. Watson in chapter 1, lines 1 to 10 in The Sign of Four?"

"I know! I know! But I've got only one peremptory left!"

"Mr. Sizemore...your 11 o'clock...that small businessman...has just arrived."

"Do you seriously expect us to believe that you would consider voting against the death penalty?"

CIVIL & CRIMINAL PROCED.
CONTRACTS
TORTS
LAW OF THE JUNGLE
LAW OF THE JUNGLE

"You tell her that I'm willing to give up the house, the boat, the car, the expresso machine and the cat, but that I'm NOT willing to give up my conjugal rights!"

"Your Honor, my client, Dorothea Pennington von Furstenberg isn't here for her Court-ordered appearance owing to a previous engagement, but she does send you her regards and will, of course, have her people call you to reschedule."

"FDR failed miserably when he tried to 'pack the Court' but Harvard and Yale didn't."

Eight of the nine current Supreme Court justices graduated from either Harvard or Yale Law School and the ninth, Ruth Ginsburg, attended Harvard Law School her first two years.

"Yeah, I miss the law...but what I miss most are the fees."

"...and now, let me call your attention to Exhibit A, the actual murder weapon."

"Uuhh...yes, Your Honor, I have been previously disbarred, but only once and only in this state."

"I've been a professional pet for most of my working life, and I've been a pretty darned good one, by the way."

"Most of the people here are lawyers, and I've been dying to ask you...what line of business are you in?"

"My client says he's not guilty, but I don't believe him."

"Ladies and Gentlemen of the Jury...I'm not going to talk about my client's poverty, nor about his destitute background, nor about the countless abuses he endured during most of his childhood, nor about the lousy education he received, nor about all of the injustices he has suffered at the hands of our heartless society and justice system...no...I'm not going to say one solitary word about any of these things because that might be construed as pandering."

"...and do you further swear to tell the truth, the whole truth and nothing but the truth so help you God?"

"You remind me of my husband...he's always asking me all these really stupid questions."

"Despite overwhelming direct evidence and numerous eye–witness accounts, we find the Defendant NOT GUILTY. Quite frankly, we rather like him."

ROCKS
DON'T KILL
PEOPLE
PEOPLE KILL
PEOPLE
ARAGÓN
&
GUERREROS-©

"Your Honor, the charge of Murder should be summarily dismissed. As the so-called 'victim' believed in 'Life Everlasting,' he is, technically speaking, not dead."

"Your Honor, we want to thank the Prosecution and Defense for a most entertaining trial. Guys, we really enjoyed it. Kudos to you, Judge Paul, for being such a charming and witty host."

"Your Honor, if I may, but isn't twenty years to life somewhat severe for a simple parking violation?"

"Your Honor, Defense would now like to call upon its principal character witness."

"I may be old fashioned, but I just thought they needed 'killin'."

"You want reasons? I'll give you reasons! If you don't acquit my client, you're gonna get your legs broken!"

"All of them! Every last one of them!"

"Your Honor, though the Defendant has the right to be judged by his peers, isn't this going a bit too far?"

"Your Honor, I know this sounds really weird, but the Jury thinks you're the one who's guilty."

"Lemme' get this straight...I'm suing you for unpaid legal fees and you want to retain me to defend you?"

"I've giving you a ten year sentence, with eight years credit for time spent in marriage."

"We're going to pause for a brief commercial time out, but we'll be right back after these messages."

"If you don't have something nice to say about someone, don't say anything at all!"

"When you referred to Defendant as 'a helluva guy,' precisely what did you mean?"

"'Members of the Jury, these are my instructions: First, no chewing gum unless you brought enough for everybody. Second, you will adhere strictly to the princple of 'one man, one vote,' which means that women on the jury will not be voting at this time. Finally, the foreman will be provided with a set of scales so that you may carefully weigh the evidence."

"If elected, I would allow anyone to purchase a handgun, but I wouldn't allow anyone to purchase ammunition."

"Your Honor, we jurors believe that humans are nothing more than pawns in the game of life, which makes us wonder if anyone is ever truly guilty."

"Please give the Court your full name, occupation and place of business."

"The Ten Commandments? Why not just call it the Bill of Wrongs?"

"I'm throwing out the charges of Murder in the First Degree but only because we're neighbors, but don't you EVER do anything like that again, you hear!"

"Your attorney doesn't seem to know what the hell he's doing...where in the world did you find this guy?"

"Yeah, I killed him. I'm a Killer Bee, for crissakes!"

"...so then they arrested me for possession of grass. Now I've got a Court date on the 9th that I can't possibly make cause I'm supposed to be slaughtered on the 6th!"

"I just enrolled…how soon can I start to take courses in billing?"

"Of course I'm upset! Except for the murder weapon, DNA match, signed confession and numerous eyewitness accounts the prosecution had no case."

"Hold on there, Judge! I'm the one asking the questions."

"You understand, of course, that as a Junior Associate of Doberman and Millbank, your hours will be 24/7/365."

MY SON IS A MODEL PRISIONER AT THE CALIFORNIA MEN'S PENAL COLONY
ARAGÓN & GUERREROS ©

"Your Honor! He's badgering the witness!"

"Look, Freddie, they're gonna' use this theory of implied liability against me, but I'll tellya' why it's not gonna' work...it says here in the Code of Civil Procedure..."

"I'm not readin' you your rights because you don't have any."

"Noted screen writer Harry Larsen has been charged with the ratings-driven murder of leading fictional character Heather Simpson in the ninth episode of the wildly popular Desperate Cheerleaders. Said Vickie Darling, who played the part, 'He had no right to kill me!'"

"Remember, I didn't say YOU had a good case; I said I had a good case."

"At the luncheon, all the girls were talking about their lawyers, and I finally had to tell them that Carl and I didn't have even one. It was so embarrassing!"

ALL SUBPOENAED WITNESSES ARE REQUIRED TO WASH THEIR MOUTHS OUT WITH SOAP AFTER TESTIFYING
SOAP
ARAGÓN & GUERREROS ©

"No! You may not have a 'sidebar' with the jury!"

"Your Honor, how can you possibly deny bail? OK, so she was driving with an expired license, but for God's sake, man, she's your wife!"

"My client knows he must go to prison, but he'd like to take his staff with him."

"Adams, Adams and Adams...how may I connect you...
Mr. Adams? Sorry, we have no one here by that name."

"Honey, are you absolutely sure we picked the right firm?"

"...so then the judge offered me the choice between 30 years and life. I chose life...I figured it'd be shorter."

"What in God's name were you thinking! Now you will, at your expense, fully restore the Museum of Natural History's Woolly Mammoth Exhibit!"

"This verdict is very important to me... I've got this book deal lined up... you know... the inside story... and I need a verdict that's like marketable."

"I'm running late for Court, so just give it a good cleaning and leave everything exactly as you find it."

"I've got news for you, Counselor, there is no higher court!"

"Your Honor, is it really necessary to swear in this witness?"

"Your Honor, I should forewarn you that my client normally gets paid for personal appearances."

"...so like I was tellin' you, this guy is a lawyer...he's handsome, cool, really smart and he works for the government as a persecutor or something."

"The Jury finds the Defendant, my cousin Jimmy 'the Brute' O'Brien, NOT GUILTY on all counts of aggravated assault with deadly intent."

"Your Honor, the Jury would like to propose a change of venue to the Bahamas."

"Great idea! Business is bound to pick up."

"Shhh...yeah, they just got here...no, I don't know how much they got on 'em."

"In the absence of a court interpreter, the charge that my client 'created a public nuisance in a crowded mall' should be summarily dismissed."

"My client regrets the ridicule his incompetence has brought upon the criminal profession, and if acquitted, will be more circumspect in any future criminal activity."

"...and Candice, don't forget to bill them for the time it takes you to bill them."

"The Emergency motion? Of course I know where it is... it's somewhere on my desk."

"We won on every point...so we are now in complete control of our destiny."

"I don't have a problem with legalities, regulations and what-not, as long as they don't interfere with business."

Eight of nine current Supreme Court justices graduated from either Harvard or Yale Law School, and the ninth, Justice Ginsburg, attended Harvard Law School her first two years.

LAW LIBRARY

NO SMOKING
NO FOOD
TRUE ROMANCE
CONTRACTS
TORTS
SPORT
ARAGON

"As Junior Associates of Winthrop, Carruthers, Shepherd and Beagle, your hours will be 24/7/365. What you do with your free time is up to you."

"Yes, Melinda, we do celebrate these so-called 'holidays' but around here, we call them non-billable days."

"The Tax Reform Act of 1997 provided that..."

"Daddy...can you tell me again about the tax cuts?"

"Is it ok if Defendant's mother sits in on Jury deliberations?"

"They say that possession is nine-tenths of the law. Well, this is the other tenth!"

"...and don't you dare appeal this decision!"

"Let me remind you that you are still under oath and ask you, once again, why haven't you paid my legal fees?"

"Jurors 7, 9 and 11 want the 12 volumes of sworn testimony re-read...the rest of them want pillows."

"If it's unanimous for guilt, go tell Jurors 3, 7 and 9 that I want my money back!"

"The Senior Partner told be he wants less bark and more bite!"

"Your Honor, with respect to Defendant's multiple personalities, we find Tiffany, Preston and Harold not guilty, but we find overwhelming evidence as to the guilt of Bonaparte, Julia and The Almighty."

"If it's justice you want, you've come to the wrong place! This is a court of law!"

Robert J Aragon is a humorist living in the Los Angeles area. He is a graduate of UCLA and Harvard Business School and a former business executive and entrepreneur.

His artist collaborator is Rodrigo Guerrero Suarez, an award winning artist and former cartoonist for Dinero, Colombia's leading financial publication. He is a graduate of the Universidad Catolica and Escuela de Bellas Artes.